THANKFUL CAT JOURNAL

DATE:_________________________

TODAY I'M THANKFUL FOR:

1
2
3

THE BEST PART OF MY DAY...

TODAY, MY EMOTIONAL

TODAY I'M THANKFUL FOR:

1
2
3

THE BEST PART OF MY DAY...

TODAY, MY EMOTIONAL

TODAY I'M THANKFUL FOR:

1
2
3

THE BEST PART OF MY DAY...

TODAY, MY EMOTIONAL

TODAY I'M THANKFUL FOR:

1
2
3

THE BEST PART OF MY DAY...

TODAY, MY EMOTIONAL

DATE:_______________________

TODAY I'M THANKFUL FOR:

1 ____________________________
2 ____________________________
3 ____________________________

THE BEST PART OF MY DAY...

TODAY, MY EMOTIONAL

TODAY I'M THANKFUL FOR:

1
2
3

THE BEST PART OF MY DAY...

TODAY, MY EMOTIONAL

TODAY I'M THANKFUL FOR:

1
2
3

THE BEST PART OF MY DAY...

TODAY, MY EMOTIONAL

TODAY I'M THANKFUL FOR:

1
2
3

THE BEST PART OF MY DAY...

TODAY, MY EMOTIONAL

TODAY I'M THANKFUL FOR:

1
2
3

THE BEST PART OF MY DAY...

TODAY, MY EMOTIONAL

DATE: ___________________

TODAY I'M THANKFUL FOR:

1
2
3

THE BEST PART OF MY DAY...

TODAY, MY EMOTIONAL

TODAY I'M THANKFUL FOR:

1
2
3

THE BEST PART OF MY DAY...

TODAY, MY EMOTIONAL

TODAY I'M THANKFUL FOR:

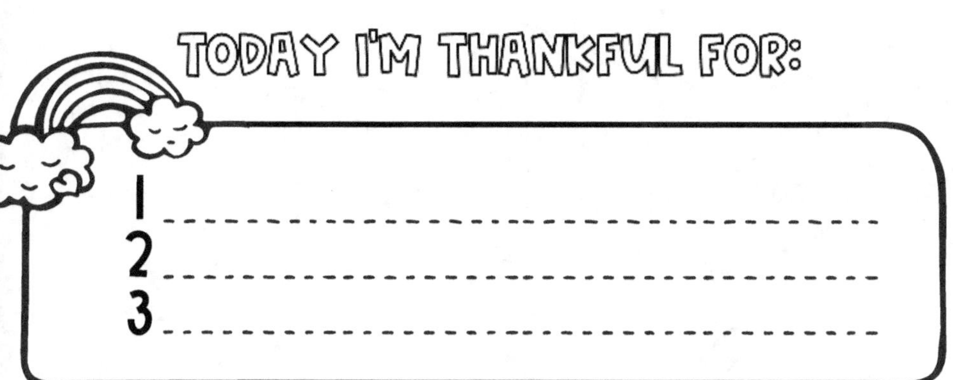

1
2
3

THE BEST PART OF MY DAY...

TODAY, MY EMOTIONAL

TODAY I'M THANKFUL FOR:

1
2
3

THE BEST PART OF MY DAY...

TODAY, MY EMOTIONAL

TODAY I'M THANKFUL FOR:

1
2
3

THE BEST PART OF MY DAY...

TODAY, MY EMOTIONAL

TODAY I'M THANKFUL FOR:

1
2
3

THE BEST PART OF MY DAY...

TODAY, MY EMOTIONAL

DATE: ________________

TODAY I'M THANKFUL FOR:

1
2
3

THE BEST PART OF MY DAY...

TODAY, MY EMOTIONAL

DATE: __________________

TODAY I'M THANKFUL FOR:

1
2
3

THE BEST PART OF MY DAY...

TODAY, MY EMOTIONAL

DATE:_____________________

TODAY I'M THANKFUL FOR:

1
2
3

THE BEST PART OF MY DAY...

TODAY, MY EMOTIONAL

TODAY I'M THANKFUL FOR:

1 ....
2 ....
3 ....

THE BEST PART OF MY DAY...

....

....

....

....

....

TODAY, MY EMOTIONAL

H₃C
CH₂
N
H₃C
H₃C

DATE:_________________

TODAY I'M THANKFUL FOR:

1
2
3

THE BEST PART OF MY DAY...

TODAY, MY EMOTIONAL

TODAY I'M THANKFUL FOR:

1
2
3

THE BEST PART OF MY DAY...

TODAY, MY EMOTIONAL

TODAY I'M THANKFUL FOR:

THE BEST PART OF MY DAY...

TODAY, MY EMOTIONAL

TODAY I'M THANKFUL FOR:

1 _______________________________
2 _______________________________
3 _______________________________

THE BEST PART OF MY DAY...

____
____
____
____
____

TODAY, MY EMOTIONAL

ART
DESIGN
HOME
POP ART
LOVE

DATE: _______________

TODAY I'M THANKFUL FOR:

1
2
3

THE BEST PART OF MY DAY...

TODAY, MY EMOTIONAL

TODAY I'M THANKFUL FOR:

1 ______________________________
2 ______________________________
3 ______________________________

THE BEST PART OF MY DAY...

____
____
____
____
____

TODAY, MY EMOTIONAL

D E
-SI-
G N

TODAY I'M THANKFUL FOR:

1
2
3

THE BEST PART OF MY DAY...

TODAY, MY EMOTIONAL

Music
Note

DATE: _______________________

TODAY I'M THANKFUL FOR:

1 _______________________
2 _______________________
3 _______________________

THE BEST PART OF MY DAY...

____
____
____
____
____

TODAY, MY EMOTIONAL

TODAY I'M THANKFUL FOR:

1
2
3

THE BEST PART OF MY DAY...

TODAY, MY EMOTIONAL

TODAY I'M THANKFUL FOR:

1 ______________________________
2 ______________________________
3 ______________________________

THE BEST PART OF MY DAY...

____
____
____
____
____

TODAY, MY EMOTIONAL

HAPPY
BIRTHDAY
TO YOU

TODAY I'M THANKFUL FOR:

1
2
3

THE BEST PART OF MY DAY...

TODAY, MY EMOTIONAL